96 FACTS ABOUT CAITLIN CLARK

Quizzes, QUOTES, QUESTIONS, and MORE!

BY ARIE KAPLAN
ILLUSTRATED BY Risa Rodil

Grosset & Dunlap

GROSSET & DUNLAP
An imprint of Penguin Random House LLC
1745 Broadway, New York, New York 10019

First published in the United States of America by Grosset & Dunlap,
an imprint of Penguin Random House LLC, 2025

Text copyright © 2025 by Arie Kaplan, LLC
Illustrations copyright © 2025 by Risa Rodil

Photo credits: used throughout: (speech bubbles with question marks)
Oleksandr Melnyk/iStock/Getty Images

Penguin Random House values and supports copyright. Copyright fuels creativity, encourages diverse voices, promotes free speech, and creates a vibrant culture. Thank you for buying an authorized edition of this book and for complying with copyright laws by not reproducing, scanning, or distributing any part of it in any form without permission. You are supporting writers and allowing Penguin Random House to continue to publish books for every reader. Please note that no part of this book may be used or reproduced in any manner for the purpose of training artificial intelligence technologies or systems.

GROSSET & DUNLAP is a registered trademark of
Penguin Random House LLC.

Visit us online at penguinrandomhouse.com.

Manufactured in Canada

ISBN 9798217051076   10 9 8 7 6 5 4 3 2 1 FRI

Design by Kimberley Sampson

The publisher does not have any control over and does not assume any responsibility for author or third-party websites or their content.

The authorized representative in the EU for product safety and compliance is Penguin Random House Ireland, Morrison Chambers, 32 Nassau Street, Dublin D02 YH68, Ireland, https://eu-contact.penguin.ie.

TABLE OF CONTENTS

Part I
Finding Focus 4

Part II
Her High-School Career 20

Part III
Go Hawkeyes! 36

Part IV
Courtside Creativity and
Charitable Contributions 52

Part V
Boundless Horizons 68

FINDING FOCUS

A True Icon

In April 2024, the mega-talented basketball player Caitlin Clark was selected as the top pick in the WNBA draft by the Indiana Fever. Prior to that, Caitlin had spent the past four years meticulously building one of the greatest college basketball careers in the history of the sport. She is famous for her playmaking prowess, her scoring skills, and her tendency to set—and break—numerous records.

But that's Caitlin Clark, the athlete. Who is Caitlin Clark, the person? When did she discover that she loved basketball? And was it difficult for her to go from college superstar to WNBA player? What was that journey like?

Read on to discover the answers to these questions, and many others!

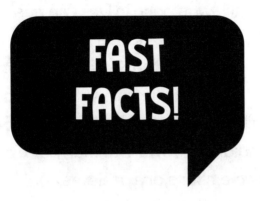

Caitlin's Zodiac sign is Aquarius.

And she's six feet tall.

An Athletic Family

Caitlin Clark was born in Des Moines, Iowa, on January 22, 2002. Her mother's name is Anne Nizzi-Clark, and her father's name is Brent Clark. Brent was a four-year letter winner in basketball and baseball, both of which he played at Simpson College in Indianola, Iowa. But many of Caitlin's *other* family members are athletes, too!

For instance, Caitlin's older brother, Blake, played football at Iowa State University. Her younger brother, Colin, participated in both basketball and track and field while in high school. And one of her cousins, Audrey Faber, played college basketball for Creighton University.

Even Caitlin's uncles are athletes! One of them, Tom Faber, played basketball at Drake University and Utica College.

And another uncle, Mike Nizzi, played college football for the University of Nebraska Omaha.

So Many Sports!

When Caitlin was around two or three years old, her parents realized that she had unusually advanced motor skills. And throughout her childhood, Caitlin was uniquely energetic and fiercely competitive. With this in mind, Caitlin's parents enrolled her in numerous activities, including soccer, softball, volleyball, basketball, and tennis.

However, Caitlin wasn't the most patient child, and she soon became frustrated with some sports, like softball, which required each player to wait their turn. She realized that basketball was more her speed.

When Caitlin and her brothers were growing up, they used to play basketball together in their driveway and basement.

During those same years, Caitlin and her family would often go out to watch local basketball games or tournaments.

All Iowa Attack Basketball

When Caitlin was in the sixth grade, she joined a program called All Iowa Attack Basketball. The program was part of the Nike Elite Youth Basketball League, or Nike EYBL, which is a group of amateur and student leagues. The coaches at All Iowa Attack Basketball taught Caitlin how to pass, how to shoot, and how to dribble correctly. In other words, they taught her the skills she would need if she wanted to play basketball on the college level.

FAST FACTS!

Caitlin was in the seventh grade when she really began impressing the folks running All Iowa Attack Basketball.

That's because they noticed that she was good enough to compete against ninth graders.

Did You Know That...

1 When Caitlin was in grade school, she sometimes played in boys' recreational basketball leagues.

2 That's because there weren't very many opportunities for girls in that part of the country in those days.

3 Caitlin's mom, Anne, is a marketing executive.

4 Caitlin has said that her mother is one of her best friends.

5 And her dad, Brent, is the executive vice president at an agricultural industrial equipment company.

6 Brent was one of Caitlin's first-ever basketball coaches when she was a kid.

7 Caitlin's maternal grandfather, Bob Nizzi, was a football coach at Dowling Catholic High School.

8 That's where Caitlin and her brothers attended high school.

9 Caitlin's older brother, Blake, won two state titles in football while at Dowling.

10 Her younger brother, Colin, won a state title in track (also while at Dowling).

Your Support System

"I'm very grateful and very thankful to be surrounded by so many people that have kind of been my foundation with everything that I've done since I was a young little girl."

—**Caitlin on the people who've helped her throughout her life**

The people who've helped and guided you throughout your life are your support system. Your "foundation," so to speak. Who makes up *your* support system? Which friends, family members, mentors, and other people have supported and guided you? Write about your support system on the lines below.

_____
_____
_____
_____
_____
_____
_____
_____
_____
_____
_____
_____
_____
_____
_____
_____
_____

Which One Do You Prefer?

As mentioned earlier in this book, when Caitlin was a child, she played many sports, including soccer, softball, volleyball, basketball, and tennis. Do you enjoy playing a particular sport? Which one do you like the best? Are you on a team? What position do you play? And if the answer to all of these questions so far is "no" or "none of them," which sport *would* you like to play, if given the chance?

_____
_____
_____
_____
_____
_____
_____
_____
_____
_____
_____
_____
_____
_____
_____
_____

Quiz: Dunking and Dreaming

1) Caitlin's middle name is ____.

   a. Abby Cadabby
   b. Alice Snuffleupagus
   c. Meryl Sheep
   d. Elizabeth

2) Caitlin was so good at shooting baskets that by the time she entered junior high school, she was well-known in Iowa's basketball ____.

   a. Factory
   b. Community
   c. Manufacturing plant
   d. Assembly line

3) In addition to playing basketball, Caitlin also enjoys playing ____ in her spare time.

   a. Golf
   b. The game of hover-cars
   c. The game of laser blasters
   d. The game of robo-boxing

4) Once, in the second grade, Caitlin wrote down her future goals, which included playing in the ____.

   a. Forest
   b. Creek
   c. WNBA
   d. Playground

5) When Caitlin was four years old, she figured out how to ride a ____ by watching her parents teach her six-year-old brother Blake how to do it.

   a. Horse
   b. Bike
   c. Mule
   d. Donkey

Check your answers on page 78!

HER HIGH-SCHOOL CAREER

Right out of the Gate

In the fall of 2016, Caitlin Clark began attending Dowling Catholic High School in West Des Moines, Iowa. And almost instantly after joining the school's basketball team, she proved herself an asset, averaging 15.3 points, 4.7 assists, and 2.3 steals during her freshman year.

In press interviews, Kristin Meyer, who coached Caitlin throughout her high-school basketball career, has praised Caitlin's raw talent, fearlessness, work ethic, and passion for the sport, all of which were evident even back then.

In basketball, a "steal" is when a player takes the ball away from their opponent or otherwise gains possession of the ball.

And an "assist" is when a player passes the ball to a teammate and it leads to a basket. It's called an assist because the player is directly aiding their teammate in scoring for their team.

Second in the State

During Caitlin's sophomore year, she was ranked second in the state, a feat she achieved by scoring (roughly) 27 points per game. She also led Dowling Catholic High School to an appearance at the state tournament.

At this time, the Iowa news media was taking notice of Caitlin's talent—in 2018, the *Des Moines Register* named her the CIML player of the year.

All of this would have been impressive enough if Caitlin was merely shooting hoops. However, during her freshman and sophomore years, Caitlin was on the soccer team at Dowling *as well as* the basketball team!

"CIML" stands for Central Iowa Metropolitan League.

The CIML is a high-school athletic conference which includes Dowling as one of its member schools.

Her Sixty-Point Game

In 2019, during Caitlin's junior year, she scored sixty points in a single game, which was just one point away from the state record at the time. In that game, Caitlin also hit thirteen three-pointers. At the time, this was the largest number of three-pointers ever notched in a single game in Iowa girls' basketball history.

Right after the game ended, the students who were there to cheer on the opposing team lined up to get Caitlin's autograph!

And that sixty-point game wasn't Caitlin's only accomplishment during her junior season! She also led the state in scoring.

A "three-pointer" is a basketball shot or field goal taken from behind the three-point line.

The "three-point line" is the curved line that stretches around the basket.

Ever Upward

In Caitlin's senior year, she continued to excel, averaging 33.4 points, 8.0 rebounds, 4.0 assists, and 2.7 steals per game. She also led the state in scoring for a second straight year. By the end of that year, she ranked number four in points and number six in three-pointers on the all-time scoring roster for five-on-five girls' high-school basketball in Iowa.

During her high school years, Caitlin had received scholarship offers from many different colleges. She eventually chose to play basketball for the Hawkeyes at the University of Iowa. That way, she would be close to her family!

"Five-on-five" is the type of basketball most Americans watch on television.

In a five-on-five game, the full court is utilized, as are two baskets. However, a three-on-three game is played with just one basket on a half-court.

Did You Know That . . .

1 During Caitlin's sophomore year of high school, she averaged 6.5 rebounds, 4.0 assists, and 2.3 steals per game.

2 While playing basketball for Dowling, Caitlin won numerous Gatorade Player of the Year honors.

3 When Caitlin was at Dowling, her team went to the state tournament three times.

4 The game where Caitlin scored sixty points took place on February 4, 2019.

5 As a junior, Caitlin scored an average of 32.5 points per game.

6 Caitlin's coach at Dowling has said that she got calls from college recruiters who were interested in Caitlin.

7 But the unusual thing is that she began getting those calls even *before* Caitlin's freshman year of high school began! That's how good Caitlin was!

8 At the World Cup in 2019, Caitlin won a gold medal with the Team USA U19 (under-nineteen) women's team.

9 By the time Caitlin graduated from Dowling, she'd scored a grand total of 2,547 points during her high-school basketball career.

10 She also racked up a total of 283 three-pointers during that same period.

The Best Version

"I'm trying to learn about myself. At the same time, I have to be the best version of myself. I have to be the best version of myself for my teammates, and for the fans, and for my family."

—Caitlin on her ongoing journey of self-improvement

What does it mean to be the "best version of yourself"? Does it mean to maintain a positive attitude? To help others? To have empathy? Write about it on the lines below.

Your Special Talent

Caitlin is really good at making three-pointers. What are *you* really good at doing? Drawing pictures? Writing poetry? Playing basketball? Solving math problems? Playing the guitar? Write about your special talent on the lines below.

_____
_____
_____
_____
_____
_____
_____
_____
_____
_____
_____
_____
_____
_____
_____
_____

Quiz: Working Hard and Playing Hard

1) When Caitlin played for her Dowling Catholic High School basketball team, which position did she play?

   a. Chaser
   b. Seeker
   c. Point guard
   d. Keeper

2) Caitlin was named a McDonald's ____ when she was in high school.

   a. All-American
   b. Pirate
   c. Buccaneer
   d. Corsair

3) Caitlin's former teammates from her years at Dowling have described her as a good ____ who took them under her wing.

   a. Eagle
   b. Duckling
   c. Hawk
   d. Leader

4) The basketball team Caitlin played for at Dowling Catholic High School was the ____.

   a. Dodgers
   b. Maroons
   c. Orioles
   d. Yankees

5) In 2020, Caitlin was rated number four by ____ in a "HoopGurlz" ranking of that year's graduating seniors who were girls' high-school basketball players.

   a. R2-D2
   b. C-3PO
   c. ESPN
   d. BB-8

Check your answers on page 78!

Part III

GO HAWKEYES!
A Stunning Debut

In the fall of 2020, when Caitlin Clark began attending the University of Iowa, she knew that she had a lot to prove as a newly minted college basketball player. Now she was playing for the Hawkeyes, and it was as if all she'd accomplished in high school didn't matter. How would she fare in this new stage of her athletic career?

Pretty well, as it turned out.

During her collegiate debut on November 25, 2020, Caitlin scored twenty-seven points, three treys, eight rebounds, and four assists. By the time the game was over, she'd led the Hawkeyes to a 96–81 win. By any metric, it was a good start to the season, and an excellent debut for Caitlin.

FAST FACTS!

In basketball, a "trey" is a shot which is worth three points.

And a "rebound" is a stat awarded to a player who retrieves a live ball after a missed free throw or field goal.

Confident and Secure

During Caitlin's sophomore year, she was more confident and had a greater command of the court than she had in the previous year. This was evident in her performance during her second year of college.

For instance, on January 2, 2022, she propelled the Hawkeyes to a victory (93–56) against the Evansville Purple Aces. In doing so, she racked up a whopping forty-four of the team's ninety-three points, setting a new Carver-Hawkeye Arena women's basketball record.

And in March of that year, she was named the Big Ten Conference Player of the Year, as voted on by a select group of Big Ten media members and conference coaches.

FAST FACTS!

When Caitlin was named Big Ten Conference Player of the Year, she led the nation in total assists (225), total points (743), assists per game (8.3), points per game (27.5), and triple-doubles (5).

In basketball, a "triple-double" is when a player has a double-digit score in at least three statistical categories (e.g., points, assists, and rebounds) during a game.

Find Peace in the Quest

During Caitlin's junior year at the University of Iowa—from the fall of 2022 to the spring of 2023—she worked hard to improve her attitude on the court. Before this, she'd felt pressure to succeed, to earn praise, to smash records, and to win. It was causing her anxiety, and she wasn't enjoying herself. So she decided to adopt a saying: *Find peace in the quest.* In other words, it's not about the destination. It's about the journey. Thinking about this saying helped lessen her anxiety.

Not all of Caitlin's challenges that season were psychological. In the early games of the season, she injured her ankle. But on November 20, 2022, Caitlin overcame that injury and helped the Hawkeyes take down the Belmont Bruins, 73–62.

FAST FACTS!

Even though she had an injured ankle, Caitlin scored thirty-three points during the game on November 20, 2022.

In that game, she was the only player whose score was in the double digits.

A Winning Season

Caitlin spent her senior year leading the Hawkeyes to a winning season! She averaged 31.6 points a game that year. But that wasn't Caitlin's only notable accomplishment during the 2023-2024 season. She also shattered the NCAA women's career scoring record!

As Caitlin approached the end of her senior year, she had a choice to make. She could either play college basketball for one more year, or she could see what lay beyond the confines of the University of Iowa. She chose the latter, declaring that she would be part of the 2024 WNBA draft. And in April of that year, Caitlin was chosen as the number-one pick in the draft by the Indiana Fever!

FAST FACTS!

In the world of professional sports, a "draft" is when new players are selected from a pool of potential candidates who are entering the league.

"WNBA" stands for "Women's National Basketball Association."

Did You Know That . . .

1 During Caitlin's freshman year at the University of Iowa, she led the NCAA Division I women's teams in scoring.

2 "NCAA" stands for "National Collegiate Athletic Association."

3 During her second year as a Hawkeye, Caitlin was known for making long three-point shots.

4 This soon became her signature move.

5 And when Caitlin broke the NCAA women's career scoring record, she did it with one of her famous three-point shots.

6 Then she proceeded to destroy the NCAA *men's* career scoring record!

7 Doing that made Caitlin the highest-scoring DI college basketball player in history at that time.

8 "DI" means "Division I."

9 Division I is the top part, or division, of the NCAA.

10 On December 6, 2023, Caitlin became the fifteenth player in the history of Division I women's basketball to reach 3,000 points throughout her career.

Achieving Your Dreams

"I want my legacy to be the impact that I have on young kids and the people in the state of Iowa. I hope I brought them a lot of joy this season.... I was just that young girl, so all you have to do is dream, and you can be in moments like this."

—Caitlin on achieving your dreams

From a young age, Caitlin dreamed of being a professional basketball player. What do you want to do for a living when you're an adult? What's *your* dream? Do you want to be a doctor? A teacher? An artist? An athlete? A musician? Write about your dreams on the lines below.

_____
_____
_____
_____
_____
_____
_____
_____
_____
_____
_____
_____
_____
_____
_____
_____
_____
_____

Dealing with Anxiety

For a time, Caitlin felt anxiety about playing basketball. Then she changed the way she thought about playing the game, and that made her feel more at ease. Has there ever been a time when you felt anxiety about something? What helped you deal with the source of your anxiety? Were your friends and family members able to help you? Write about it on the lines below.

_____
_____
_____
_____
_____
_____
_____
_____
_____
_____
_____
_____
_____
_____
_____
_____
_____

Quiz: College Life

1) When Caitlin was at the University of Iowa, her favorite basketball hero was Maya Moore of the Minnesota ____.

   a. Basketball Playing Team
   b. Lynx
   c. Athletic Folks
   d. Sporty People

2) Ever since she began playing for the Hawkeyes, Caitlin's ____ number has been twenty-two.

   a. Jersey
   b. Favorite
   c. Least favorite
   d. Second-most favorite

3) During Caitlin's college years, she became such a big basketball star that she signed endorsement deals with Nike, State Farm, and ____.

   a. Happy Kid's Funtime Palace
   b. Happy Kid's Funtime Castle
   c. Happy Kid's Funtime Mansion
   d. Gatorade

4) In January 2024, shortly before Caitlin's twenty-second birthday, her fellow Hawkeyes threw her an early celebration with two cakes and ____.

   a. A magical sword
   b. A magical helmet
   c. Confetti
   d. A magical shield

5) When Caitlin is on the court, arms ____, radiating positivity—that's often considered the classic "Caitlin Clark" pose.

   a. Outstretched
   b. Wiggling and pointing upward
   c. Wiggling and pointing downward
   d. Wiggling and pointing every which way

Check your answers on page 78!

Part IV

COURTSIDE CREATIVITY AND CHARITABLE CONTRIBUTIONS

Adjusting and Excelling

Shortly after Caitlin joined the Indiana Fever, some people mused that she might have trouble adjusting to a league full of players who were more experienced and mature than those she'd known in college. But if there was a difficult transitional period, it was a minimal one because soon, she proved that she lived up to the hype.

For instance, on June 7, 2024, Caitlin led the Fever to a win against the Washington Mystics in a courtside performance the *Washington Post* called "The Caitlin Clark Show."

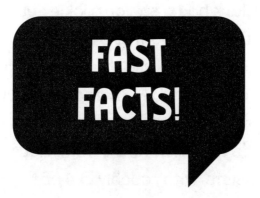

During the June 7 game, the Fever beat the Mystics, 85-83.

And thirty of those eighty-five points were racked up by Caitlin.

A Stellar Season

Caitlin Clark had a stellar rookie season. During her first few months playing with the Indiana Fever, she became the quickest rookie in the history of the WNBA to reach one hundred points and fifty assists.

But that's not all. In 2024, Caitlin led the WNBA in assists, with roughly 8.4 of them per game. More importantly, she also had a combined total of 337 assists in her 2024 rookie season, shattering the WNBA record for assists in a single season by *any* player, rookie or otherwise.

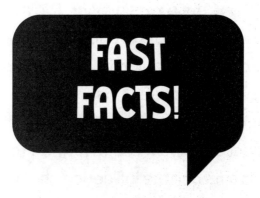

In the summer of 2024, *Sports Illustrated* called Caitlin one of the WNBA's best passers.

In basketball, a "passer" is someone who throws the ball to another player on the team.

The Caitlin Clark Effect

Back when Caitlin was playing for the Hawkeyes, women's basketball had started to see an explosion in popularity. Caitlin was one of the people who *caused* this explosion. She brought more fans to arenas, bigger audiences to TV broadcasts, and more attention to games in general. Some call the influence she has had on her chosen sport "The Caitlin Clark Effect."

This effect had continued during Caitlin's rookie year with the Indiana Fever. Her star power, dynamic scoring ability, and courtside creativity had caused attendance rates for Fever games to go up by an astonishing 265 percent.

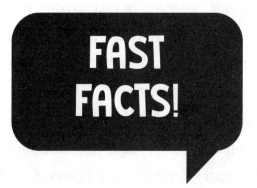

During Caitlin's rookie year, Fever jersey sales went up by 1,193 percent.

And the Fever's social media following had increased by over 1.3 million since Caitlin began playing for the team.

The Caitlin Clark Foundation

Caitlin Clark believes in using her platform to help others. That's why, in 2021, shortly after her freshman basketball season, she partnered with the Coralville Community Food Pantry, a charitable organization that gives food to those in need. Together, Caitlin and the Coralville Community Food Pantry raised over $100,000.

Then in 2023, Caitlin took things to the next level by founding her own nonprofit company called the Caitlin Clark Foundation. This philanthropic organization's goal is to improve the lives of kids and the communities in which they live, through nutrition, education, and sports programs. Caitlin has said that—through her foundation—she wants to give other kids the same opportunities for success that she had as a child.

Caitlin didn't want to be paid for her work with the Iowa-based Coralville Community Food Pantry.

She didn't want to take any resources—including money—away from her fellow Iowans.

Did You Know That...

1 In April 2024, shortly after Caitlin was chosen as the first pick in the WNBA draft by the Indiana Fever, she received a surprise video message congratulating her.

2 The message was from country music legend Luke Combs, who is Caitlin's favorite musician.

3 In the 2023–2024 season, for the first time ever, the NCAA women's basketball championship drew more viewers than the men's championship.

4 And according to *NPR*, Caitlin Clark's popularity was a large part of the reason why the viewership surged during that season.

5 By the time the mid-season break began—on July 21, 2024—the Indiana Fever were the most-viewed team in the WNBA.

6 The team boasted ten broadcasts which broke viewership records.

7 During Caitlin's rookie season, the Indiana Fever also set records for the most-watched games on ESPN, ION, ABC, and NBA TV.

8 One of those games was the most-viewed WNBA game (overall) in more than two decades.

9 According to *Sports Illustrated*, Caitlin is the most popular women's basketball player in the history of the sport.

10 In a 2024 interview, Caitlin revealed that she was obsessed with the Hasbro card game Monopoly Deal.

Back in Time

"I haven't really had time to reflect, I'll probably save that for the off-season. I wish I could go back in time and relive it through a different perspective, watching from a bird's eye view."

—Caitlin talking about the hectic nature of her rookie season with the Indiana Fever

Does it ever seem like time passes by *super quickly*? Sometimes, it's hard to keep up! If you had a time machine and could go back to one specific moment in your life, what moment would it be? On the lines below, describe that moment and explain why it's important to you.

_____
_____
_____
_____
_____
_____
_____
_____
_____
_____
_____
_____
_____
_____
_____
_____
_____
_____
_____
_____

Giving to Others

As we discussed earlier in this book, Caitlin likes working with charitable organizations. Have you ever given money to charity? Have you worked as a volunteer for a philanthropic (that means "charitable") organization? What was that experience like? Is there a particular charity you'd like to work with in the future? Is there a charitable cause you feel strongly about? Write about it on the lines below.

Quiz: Achievements and Altruism

1) In both the University of Iowa Hawkeyes and the Indiana Fever, Caitlin held (and continues to hold) the same position: ____ ____.

   a. Point guard
   b. Clarinet player
   c. Cowbell player
   d. Bass player

2) In August 2024, NBA legend Isaiah Thomas took to X (formerly Twitter) to point out Caitlin's uncanny ability to both score and ____ at an equally high rate.

   a. Do card tricks
   b. Separate linked metal rings
   c. Assist
   d. Pull a rabbit out of a hat

3) In the summer of 2024, the Iowa State Fair honored Caitlin by making a life-size sculpture of her out of ____.

   a. Basketballs
   b. Butter
   c. Basketball hoops
   d. Basketball jerseys

4) In 2024, Caitlin launched her own breakfast cereal, Caitlin's Crunch ____, and the proceeds went to the Caitlin Clark Foundation.

   a. Porridge
   b. Time
   c. Oatmeal
   d. Grits

5) In addition to her work with other charities, Caitlin has given money to The Boys and Girls Clubs of Central ____.

   a. Mars
   b. Venus
   c. Saturn
   d. Iowa

Check your answers on page 78!

Part V

BOUNDLESS HORIZONS

Making History

On Friday, August 16, 2024, Caitlin came back from the mid-season break and began the second half of her rookie season with the Indiana Fever by helping her team score a 98-89 win over the Phoenix Mercury.

But in doing so, Caitlin broke yet another record. She became the *first* player in WNBA history to score at least 450 points in her *rookie* season. There are only five other WNBA players in the league's history who could boast that achievement during *any other* season of their careers. By the end of the 2024 season, Caitlin had set a new rookie record by scoring 769 points in a single season.

Also in August 2024, Caitlin became the record-holder for most three-pointers by a WNBA rookie.

By the end of the 2024 season, Caitlin had made 122 three-pointers.

The Future Looks Bright

Currently, Caitlin Clark is an acclaimed and celebrated athlete. Journalist Robin Lundberg has labeled her the best point guard in the WNBA. And WNBA icon Rebecca Lobo has said that Caitlin is the best passer in the league today.

But where will Caitlin Clark go from here? What sort of a basketball career will she have going forward?

It's impossible to tell at this point. But one thing is for certain: The future looks bright for Caitlin!

FAST FACTS!

In basketball, a "point guard" is the person who is responsible for keeping the ball in their team's possession and creating opportunities for the team to score, acting as a sort of team leader or "coach on the floor."

The point guard is also the player in charge of moving the ball up the court. They're expected to be really good at dribbling, ball handling, and passing.

Did You Know That...

1 In the game that took place on August 18, 2024, the Indiana Fever beat the Seattle Storm, 92–75.

2 On July 20, 2024, Caitlin Clark (of the Indiana Fever) and Angel Reese (of the Chicago Sky) teamed up against the US Olympic women's basketball team in the WNBA All-Star Game in Phoenix, Arizona.

3 At the All-Star Game, Caitlin and Angel represented Team WNBA, which won the matchup.

4 Even though Caitlin and Angel play for different teams and some fans think they're rivals, they're actually friendly.

5 On Saturday, April 13, 2024, Caitlin made a surprise appearance on the sketch comedy series *Saturday Night Live*.

6 The appearance happened during the show's "Weekend Update" segment, a parody of TV news broadcasts.

7 Before Caitlin appeared, "Update" anchor Michael Che told a joke about her.

8 Then Caitlin appeared and told Michael to read some jokes about himself which *she* had written.

9 After Michael read the jokes, Caitlin delivered a heartfelt message in which she thanked some of the great WNBA players who had come before her.

10 The players she thanked in her message were Sheryl Swoopes, Lisa Leslie, Cynthia Cooper, Dawn Staley, and Maya Moore.

Responsibility

"I'm twenty-two years old, and there's a lot of expectations on my shoulders. I feel like I've grown a lot, and I'm going to continue to grow. Allowing myself a lot of grace at times is really hard because I'm a perfectionist and I want to be really good for our organization, for my teammates. And I've done some really good stuff, but also I've learned a lot, too."

—Caitlin talking about personal growth and managing expectations

Caitlin has said that people expect a lot out of her as a professional athlete. That must be a huge responsibility, and it can't be easy. Has there ever been a time when someone expected a lot from you? Was there a time when you had a big responsibility to do something? What was at stake? How did you handle it? Did anyone help you? Write about it on the lines below.

_____
_____
_____
_____
_____
_____
_____
_____
_____
_____
_____
_____
_____
_____
_____
_____
_____
_____

Your Heroes

In 2024, Caitlin spoke about her WNBA heroes when she appeared on *Saturday Night Live*. Who are *your* heroes? Are they world leaders? Activists? Movie stars? Athletes? Pop stars? Write about your personal heroes on the lines below.

_____
_____
_____
_____
_____
_____
_____
_____
_____
_____
_____
_____
_____
_____
_____

ANSWER KEY

Pages 18–19:
1) d, 2) b, 3) a, 4) c, 5) b

Pages 34–35:
1) c, 2) a, 3) d, 4) b, 5) c

Pages 50–51:
1) b, 2) a, 3) d, 4) c, 5) a

Pages 66–67:
1) a, 2) c, 3) b, 4) b, 5) d

ABOUT THE AUTHOR

Arie Kaplan is a *USA Today* bestselling author who has written many nonfiction books, including *From Krakow to Krypton: Jews and Comic Books*; *American Pop: Hit Makers, Superstars, and Dance Revolutionaries*; *Swashbuckling Scoundrels: Pirates in Fact and Fiction*; and *The Encyclopedia of Epic Myths and Legends: Extraordinary and Mesmerizing Stories That Will Boggle Your Mind*.

Arie has also penned numerous books and graphic novels for young readers, including *Jurassic Park Little Golden Book*, *Frankie and the Dragon*, *LEGO Star Wars: The Official Stormtrooper Training Manual*, *The New Kid from Planet Glorf*, *Batman: Harley at Bat!*, *Spider-Man Comictivity*, *Shadow Guy and Gamma Gal: Heroes Unite*, and *Speed Racer: Chronicles of the Racer*. In addition, he is a screenwriter for television, video games, and transmedia. Please check out his website: www.ariekaplan.com.